CREATING A CULTURE OF ENGAGEMENT
Selling Strategies for Improving Employee Retention

Brad Young PhD
Michael Hanks

CREATING A CULTURE OF ENGAGEMENT
Selling Strategies for Improving Employee Retention
Copyright © 2022 by The Self Development Factory Inc

ISBN: 979-8-88831-501-9

DEDICATION

Hardworking individuals are the backbone of any successful organization. They put in tireless hours to keep things running smoothly and provide quality service, but they can always do more! This book is dedicated specifically for you—the individual who understands there's room on your odometer just waiting until someone turns it over with hard work; dedication like yours makes all other differences invisible when compared against long days at their job.

In our society built around competition rather than collaboration or cooperation (often through automation), sometimes one person stands out among hundreds by being really good at what he/she does while simultaneously achieving something more significant.

TABLE OF CONTENTS

Foreword 7

Preface...11

Introduction 15

Chapter ONE: CONCEPTS in the book....................................19

CHAPTER TWO: HOW can I use this information? 27

Chapter Three: PROBLEM We are solving.............................35

Chapter Four: WHY is this a problem?..................................39

Chapter five: CREATING The Change 45

Chapter Six: THE Importance of Relationship Building 59

Chapter seven: THE Importance of Building Trust 67

Chapter eight: THE Importance of Creating the Right
Atmosphere 73

Chapter nine: THE Importance of Moving Away from
Authoritarian Leadership...87

Chapter ten: THE Importance of Improving Listening Skills 93

Chapter eleven: THE Importance of Learning Selling
Techniques..99

Chapter Twelve: THE Importance of Providing Value to
Employees 113

Chapter Thirteen: THE Importance of Adding Self-Development
Opportunities..119

Conclusion..127

FOREWORD

The high turnover rate in the United States is costly and detrimental to businesses. The average cost of turnover is 20% of an employee's salary. Furthermore, statistics show that the average turnover rate in the United States is 65%, so organizations must constantly replace employees. This cycle is expensive and disruptive to businesses. Additionally, 20% of turnover happens in the first 45 days of working in a new company.3 This is why it is essential to keep selling your employees on why they should stay with your organization. The selling techniques for retention concepts are relationship building, building trust with employees, creating the right atmosphere, backing away from authoritarian leadership, improving listening skills, learning selling techniques, providing value to employees, and adding self-development opportunities.

Organizations should focus on selling techniques to increase employee engagement and retention. By using these methods, businesses can create a more positive work environment, making employees feel valued and appreciated. Additionally, these techniques will help build trust between employees.

Utilizing selling techniques to increase employee engagement and improve retention is a guide that helps business leaders understand how to properly keep their employees. It considers everything from understanding employee turnover and why it matters to providing value and

opportunities for employees, so they stay with the

company.

PREFACE

The book starts by discussing employee turnover statistics in America and how costly it can be for businesses. It then details building relationships, creating the right atmosphere, being a good listener, and providing value to employees. Finally, it offers self-development opportunities to help employees grow within the company.

This book is different because it allows for new and innovative ways to sell to your employees. In a world where the average turnover rate is 65%, you can't afford to keep losing your employees. This book will teach you how to build relationships, trust, and the right atmosphere to keep your employees engaged and decrease turnover.

This book is perfect for business leaders who want to keep their employees happy and engaged. Utilizing selling techniques is a great way to improve retention and engagement in any company. This book is for you if you want to learn how to keep your employees happy and engaged. Utilizing selling techniques is a great way to improve retention and engagement in any company. Order your copy today!

Utilizing selling techniques to increase employee engagement and improve retention is a great way to keep your business running smoothly. You can trust them more by building relationships with employees and creating the right atmosphere for your business. Backing away from authoritarian leadership, improving listening skills, learning selling techniques, providing value to employees, and adding self-development opportunities are great ways to show your employees that you care about their development. Not only will this keep them engaged in their work, but it will also help retain them in your company for the long run.

INTRODUCTION

It's no secret that employee turnover rates in the United States are high. The average turnover rate is 65%. This means that businesses are constantly having to train new employees, which can be costly and time-consuming. Even more alarming is that 20% of turnover happens in the first 45 days of working in a new company. Therefore it's important to keep selling your employees on why they should stay.

Selling is often thought of as convincing someone to buy a product or service. However, to be successful, selling requires building a relationship with the customer – and that's true whether you're selling a product or trying to keep an employee engaged in their work.

Think about it: if you don't have a good relationship with your employees, they won't trust you and will not be engaged in their work. So how can you build better relationships with your employees?

Here are some tips:

1. Get to know them as people, not just employees. What are their interests? What motivates them? What makes them tick?

2. Build trust by being honest and transparent. Don't try to "sell" them on

things – just be open and upfront about what you're thinking and why.

3. Create the right atmosphere. Make sure your workplace is a positive, enjoyable place to be.

4. Back away from authoritarian leadership. Instead, focus on leading by example and empowering your employees to make their own decisions.

5. Improve your listening skills. Listen to what your employees say and try to understand their perspectives.

6. Learn some selling techniques. You don't have to be a salesperson to benefit from learning how to sell effectively.

Therefore, you have to keep selling your employees. The statistics don't lie- if you want to keep your company running like a well-oiled machine, you need to find ways to keep your employees engaged and prevent them from leaving. Selling techniques can be a great way to do this. By building relationships, creating the right atmosphere, and providing value to employees, you can keep them engaged and reduce turnover.

CHAPTER ONE: CONCEPTS IN THE BOOK

Concepts that help you retain employees are:

1. Relationship Building: Get to know your employees personally. Take an interest in their lives outside of work and get to know them as individuals.

2. Build Trust: Employees need to trust you to be engaged with their work. They will not be engaged if you feel like you are constantly looking over their shoulder or micromanaging them.

3. Create the Right Atmosphere: The work environment plays a big role in employee engagement. If the environment is upbeat, employees will be more likely to be engaged.

4. Back Away from Authoritarian Leadership: Employees do not respond well to dictator-style leadership. They need to feel like they have a voice and that their opinion matters.

5. Improve Listening Skills: One of the best ways to show employees that you are engaged is by listening to what they say. Active listening shows that you care about what they have to say.

6. Learn Selling Techniques: You can use selling techniques to engage employees in their work. If you can sell them the importance of their work, they will be more likely to be engaged.

7. Provide Value: Employees need to feel like their work is valuable and that they are making a difference. If they feel like their work is

making a difference, the value of your organization will increase in the eyes of the employee.

8. Add self-development opportunities into the mi, so that employees can continue to grow and improve even after they have left your organization.

Who is this book for?

This book is for anyone who wants to learn how to use selling techniques to improve employee retention and engagement. Whether you are a business owner, manager, or human resources professional, this book will give you the tools you need to keep your employees happy and engaged.

This book is not for anyone who is not interested in learning how to use selling techniques to improve employee retention and engagement. If you are not willing to try to learn these techniques, then this book is not for you.

This book teaches you how to use selling techniques to improve employee retention and engagement. You will learn how to build relationships with employees, create the right atmosphere, and provide value to employees. You will also learn about the importance of self-development opportunities for employees.

The target audience for this book is business owners, managers, and human resources professionals who want to learn how to use selling techniques to improve employee retention and engagement. This book is different because it focuses on selling techniques to enhance employee retention and engagement. Most books on this topic focus on either retention or attention, but not both. Additionally, this book looks at how to increase employee engagement and retention from a salesperson's perspective. Finally, this book provides tips and tricks for using selling.

Background

Did you know that the average turnover rate in the United States is 65%? 20% of that turnover happens in the first 45 days of working in a new company. (Bureau of Labor Statistics, 2017) This is why it's so important to keep selling your employees on why they should stay with your company. The concepts of selling techniques for retention are relationship building, building trust with employees, creating the right atmosphere, backing away from authoritarian leadership, improving listen to skills, learning selling techniques, providing value to employees, and adding self-development opportunities.

Selling isn't just about making a one-time purchase - it's about developing relationships built on trust. When you can do that with your employees, you create a foundation that will keep them engaged and motivated to stay with your company for the long run.

Building trust requires creating the right atmosphere. This starts with the way you communicate with your team. Are you open and honest? Do you listen to their concerns? Do you value their input? If you answered "no" to any of these questions, it's time to make some changes.

The authoritarian leadership style is a significant contributor to high turnover rates. Employees who feel like they're not being heard or valued are more likely to look for a job elsewhere. Try to be more open-minded and collaborative with your team to combat this. Seek their input and feedback and let them know their voices are heard.

Improving your listening skills is a great way to show employees that you value them and their opinions. When they're speaking, try to understand their point of view. This will go a long way in building trust and rapport.

To keep your employees engaged, you need to provide them with value. This can come in the form of exciting work, opportunities for growth and development, and a competitive salary and benefits package. Employees who feel like they're getting something out of their job are likelier to stick around.

CHAPTER TWO: HOW CAN I USE THIS INFORMATION?

When you're looking to add someone new to your team, it's important to remember that the hiring process is a two-way street. Just as you're evaluating candidates to see if they would be a good fit for your company, they are also considering whether or not the opportunity aligns with their career goals.

As the hiring manager, it's your job to sell the candidate on the opportunity to work for you. This means conveying why your company is a great place to work and what makes the role a unique and appealing opportunity.

Here are a few tips to help you sell the opportunity to work for your company:

1. Talk about your company culture

One of the things that candidates are looking for in a new role is a good fit with the company's culture. When you're selling the opportunity to work for your company, be sure to talk about the things that make your culture unique and appealing.

Some examples include:

-A collaborative and supportive environment

-A focus on professional development

-A fun and relaxed atmosphere

2. Highlight the growth potential

Another thing that candidates are looking for is the opportunity to grow in their careers. When you're selling the opportunity to work for your company, highlight the potential for growth and advancement.

Some examples include:

-Many opportunities for career advancement

-A clear path for professional development

-The chance to take on additional responsibilities over time

3. Focus on the company's mission

One of the things that can attract candidates to your company is a strong sense of purpose. When you're selling the opportunity to work for your company, be sure to focus on the company's mission and how the role can help further that mission.

Some examples include:

-A chance to make a difference in the world

-An opportunity to work for a company with a strong sense of purpose

4. Talk about the team

Another thing that can be appealing to candidates is the chance to work with a great team. When you're selling the opportunity to work for your company, be sure to talk about the team that they would be joining and why they would be a good fit.

Some examples include:

-A high-performing and cohesive team

-A team of people with diverse skills and backgrounds

5. Offer a competitive salary and benefits package

Of course, candidates are also looking for a competitive salary and benefits package. When you're selling the opportunity to work for your company, be sure to highlight the compensation and benefits that are on offer.

Some examples include:

-A competitive salary

-A comprehensive benefits package

-Generous vacation time

By following these tips, you can sell the opportunity to work for your company and attract top candidates.

Another highly attractive benefit is flex time.

Flex time is a system where employees are given more control over when they start and end their workday. This can be appealing to candidates who are looking for a better work-life balance.

If your company offers flex time, be sure to highlight this when you're selling the opportunity to work for you.

Companies with flex time score higher on job satisfaction surveys and have employees

that report being happier with their work-life balance.

So not only is offering flex time beneficial to your employees, it's also beneficial to your company.

When you're selling the opportunity to work for your company, be sure to highlight all the things that make it a great place to work.

CHAPTER THREE: PROBLEM WE ARE SOLVING.

It is no secret that employee turnover rates in the United States are high. In fact, the average turnover rate is 65%. This means that for every 10 employees you have, 6 of them will leave within a year. And 20% of all turnover happens in the first 45 days of working in a new company.

This is a huge problem for businesses because replacing employees costs a lot of money. Finding and train a replacement can cost up to 150% of an employee's salary. Not to mention the lost productivity while the position is vacant.

So how can you combat high turnover rates? One way is to keep selling your employees on why they should stay with your company.

In this book, we will discuss the concepts of selling techniques for retention. These include:

- Relationship building

- Building trust with employees

- Creating the right atmosphere

- Moving away from authoritarian leadership

- Improving listening skills

- Learning selling techniques

- Providing value to employees

- Adding self-development opportunities

If you can implement even a few of these techniques, you will see a significant decrease in turnover rates. And that will save your company time and money in the long run.

1. According to a study by the Society for Human Resource Management, the average cost of turnover is about 150% of an employee's salary. This means that for every ten employees you have, 6 of them will leave within a year, and it costs your company up to 150% of their salary to replace them.

2. many factors contribute to high turnover rates, but one way to combat this issue is by selling your employees on why they should stay with your company. This can be done through building relationships, creating trust, and providing value and opportunities for self-development.

3. If you can implement even a few of these techniques, you will see a significant decrease in turnover rates, saving your company time and money in the long run. Implementing these selling techniques can help improve employee engagement and create a more positive work environment for everyone.

Selling techniques are a great way to improve employee engagement and retention. By building relationships, creating trust, and providing value and opportunities for self-development, you can create a more positive work environment for everyone. These selling techniques can help improve your company's bottom line by reducing turnover rates.

CHAPTER FOUR: WHY IS THIS A PROBLEM?

As we mentioned, the turnover rate in the United States is high. And it costs businesses a lot of money each year.

Many factors contribute to high turnover rates. But some of the most common reasons employees leave are

- They don't feel valued or appreciated.

- They are not given opportunities for growth or development.

- The work environment is not positive or supportive.

- Their job is not a good fit for their skills or interests.

If you can address these issues, you will be on your way to reducing turnover rates. But it's not always easy to do. That's why we've put together this book. To give you the tools and techniques to keep your employees engaged and reduce turnover.

The average turnover rate in the United States is 65%. Of that, 20% of turnover happens in the first 45 days of working in a new company. This is expensive for businesses, as it can cost up to 150% of an employee's salary to replace them. To keep good employees, selling techniques must be used.

Selling techniques are often thought of as manipulative, but this does not have to be the case.

If done correctly, selling is about building relationships and providing value. When you sell to someone, you offer them something they want or need. To do this effectively, you must understand what they want or need and then be able to offer it to them in an appealing way.

The same principles can be applied to selling to employees. You must understand what they want and need from their job and then offer it to them in a way that will appeal to them. Doing this can build relationships, trust, and engagement with your employees, leading to improved retention rates.

Ask yourself: Where did it all start? Where are we now?

The problem of high turnover rates has been around for a long time. In fact, it is one of the oldest problems in business. It is expensive for businesses, as it can cost up to 150% of an employee's salary to replace them. To keep good employees, selling techniques must be used.

Selling techniques are often thought of as manipulative, but this does not have to be the case. If done correctly, selling is about building relationships and providing value. When you sell to someone, you offer them something they want or need. To do this effectively, you must understand what they want or need and then be able to offer it to them in an appealing way.

The same principles can be applied to selling to employees. You must understand what they want and need from their job and then offer it to them in a way that will appeal to them. Doing this can build relationships, trust, and engagement with your employees, leading to improved retention rates.

Many factors contribute to high turnover rates. One of the most common is a lack of engagement from employees. Employees are more likely to look for other opportunities when they are not engaged. This is why it is essential to keep selling to your employees and providing them with value. If you can do this, you will see improved retention rates and a decreased turnover.

Selling techniques are not commonly used in the workplace to improve employee engagement or retention. The typical turnover rate in the United States is 65%.20% of turnover happens in the first 45 days of working in a new company. Therefore, you have to keep selling your employees.

Selling techniques must be used more in the workplace to improve employee engagement.

CHAPTER FIVE: CREATING THE CHANGE

There are many things you can do to keep your employees. But we're going to focus on seven key areas:

- Relationship building

- Building trust with employees

- Creating the right atmosphere

- Moving away from authoritarian leadership

- Improving listening skills

- Learning selling techniques

- Providing value to employees

- Adding self-development opportunities

We'll go into more detail on each of these later. But first, let's examine why they are so important.

Building relationships with employees is essential because it creates a sense of trust and connection. When employees feel they can trust and connect with their superiors, they are more likely to be engaged in their work and less likely to leave the company.

Creating the right atmosphere is also crucial for employee retention. If the work environment is positive and supportive, employees are likelier to be happy in their jobs and less likely to look for new opportunities elsewhere.

Moving away from authoritarian leadership styles and towards more collaborative approaches is also essential. Employees are more likely to be engaged and stay with a company if they feel like their voices are heard and that their opinions matter.

Improving listening skills is another crucial way to keep employees engaged. When employees feel they are being listened to and their concerns are being addressed, they are less likely to look for new jobs.

Finally, providing employees value through training and development opportunities is also essential. Employees who feel like they are constantly learning and growing in their careers are more likely to stay with a company for the long haul.

The key to using selling techniques for employee retention and engagement is aligning your offering with what they need or want. You can build relationships, create the right atmosphere, provide value, add self-development opportunities, and more. Here's a closer look at each of these concepts.

Building relationships is essential for good retention and engagement rates. After all, people tend to stay with companies they feel a connection to. To build these relationships, get to know your employees personally. Learn about their goals and aspirations. Find out what makes them tick. Once you have this information, you can craft a retention strategy that will work for them.

Creating the right atmosphere is also essential. If your workplace is full of tension and negativity, it will be tough to keep employees engaged. On the other hand, a positive and supportive environment will go a long way towards helping people feel satisfied in their jobs. To create this atmosphere, focus on open communication, mutual respect, and positive reinforcement.

Providing value is another critical piece of the puzzle. Employees need to feel like they're getting something from their job besides a paycheck. When they don't feel valued, it's easy to become disengaged. To avoid this, ensure you're offering employees opportunities for growth and development. Help them see how their work is making a difference. And be generous with praise and recognition when they do something well.

Finally, don't forget about self-development. Many people stay in jobs they dislike because they don't feel like they have other options. But if you offer employees opportunities to improve their skills and knowledge, they'll be more likely to stick around. Consider offering tuition reimbursement, professional development courses, or even just access to online resources.

Using a Sense of Purpose for Retention

One of the things that can attract candidates to your company is a strong sense of purpose. In today's job market, workers are increasingly interested in finding companies that align with their personal values. In fact, a recent study found that nearly 60% of millennials would take a pay cut to work for an organization with a strong sense of purpose. For businesses, this means that having a clear purpose can be a major asset when it comes to attracting top talent. Candidates are looking for companies that are making a positive impact on the world, and they want to know that their work will be meaningful. By articulating your company's purpose and highlighting your efforts to make a difference, you can show candidates that your business is worth their time and energy. In a competitive job market, a strong sense of purpose can give you the edge you need to attract the best and brightest workers.

Ask yourself: Why is your method different?

Your method for using selling techniques to improve employee retention and engagement is different because it's tailored specifically to the needs of your employees. By getting to know them personally, you can create a retention strategy that will work for them specifically. Additionally, by creating a positive and supportive atmosphere, you can help employees feel satisfied in their jobs. Finally, by offering opportunities for growth and development, you can help employees see how their work is making a difference.

Selling techniques are often thought of as being used exclusively in a commercial setting. However, the same concepts can increase employee engagement and improve retention rates. Establishing relationships with employees, building trust, and creating the right atmosphere makes it possible to keep staff motivated and committed to their role within the company. Backing away from an authoritarian leadership style and instead implementing a more consultative approach will also help to encourage employees to stay with the company. Furthermore, by providing opportunities for self-development, employees will feel valued and motivated to continue developing their skills within the organization. By utilizing selling techniques in this way, it can significantly improve employee engagement and retention rates.

The concept of using selling techniques to improve employee engagement and retention rates is a sound one. By following the tips outlined above, it is possible to achieve great results. To build relationships with employees, it is essential to take the time to get to know them personally and to build trust. Creating the right atmosphere within the workplace is also crucial, and this can be achieved by ensuring that employees feel valued and respected. Finally, by providing opportunities for self-development, employees will be motivated to continue developing their skills within the organization. By taking these steps, it is possible to utilize selling techniques to significantly improve employee engagement and retention rates.

After reading the first chapters of this book, you have hopefully taken some time to assess your organization and how it functions. To create a more positive and productive work environment, it is important to analyze not only what you are doing wrong but also what you could be doing better.

What do we need to do first?

1. Take the time to get to know your employees personally. This includes taking an interest in their lives outside of work, and getting to know them as people, not just as cogs in a machine.

2. Build trust with your employees by being transparent and honest. Let them know your expectations and allow them to provide feedback.

3. Create the right atmosphere in the workplace. This means fostering an environment of respect, open communication, and collaboration.

4. Back away from authoritarian leadership styles and instead focus on coaching and mentoring your team members.

5. Improve your listening skills, and ensure that you take employees' concerns seriously.

6. Learn selling techniques that can be used to motivate employees and get them excited about their work.

7. Provide value to your employees by offering opportunities for growth and development.

8. Add self-development opportunities into the mix so that employees can continue to grow and improve even after they have left your organization.

By following these steps, you will be well on increasing employee engagement and improving retention rates in your organization.

CHAPTER SIX: THE IMPORTANCE OF RELATIONSHIP BUILDING

One of the most important things you can do to reduce turnover is to build relationships with your employees. When people feel they have a personal connection with their boss, they are more likely to stay with the company.

There are a few things you can do to build relationships with your employees:

- Get to know them on a personal level. Ask about their families, interests, and hobbies.

- Take an interest in their work and career goals.

- Be available when they need you. Let them know you're there for them.

- Show your appreciation for their hard work. A little recognition goes a long way.

By building relationships with your employees, you will create a sense of trust and connection. And that will go a long way toward reducing turnover.

We look at relationship building, we have to look at how do we form a relationship. To form a relationship, we must first get to know someone. This is the process of building rapport. Rapport is the basis of any good relationship. It's what allows us to trust and connect with someone. And it's essential for reducing turnover.

There are a few things you can do to build rapport with your employees:

- Get to know them on a personal level. Ask about their families, interests, and hobbies.

- Take an interest in their work and career goals.

- Be available when they need you. Let them know you're there for them.

- Show your appreciation for their hard work. A little recognition goes a long way.

By taking the time to build rapport with your employees, you will create the foundation for a strong relationship. And that will go a long way toward reducing turnover.

We have two authors for this book, and they have different backgrounds. Brad has been in the transportation and software industry for decades. While Michael has a military and manufacturing background. While the backgrounds are different, the concepts regarding relationships are universal.

When we look at relationship build and trust, this takes time. Brad has built relationships, good and evil all over the world. He manages a global workforce, and one of the big things regarding retention and relationships is seeking to understand. Miscommunication can derail any relationship that takes significant time to build, but if you remember a relationship being like a gas tank, and when the tank is complete you can lose so much fuel. You won't run out of fuel. If the tank is already low, this is the point relationship for out the window, and turnover occurs.

It is like dating someone for two weeks, and fighting occurs. There is no foundation built so the relationship ends or becomes toxic. Remember this when dealing with your employees. If you have a foundation, then the relationship we can grow. If there is no foundation and conflict begin, a turnover is waiting to happen. The main point is to build these relationships and grow them so your employees and you have a foundation.

Michael has an example that he experienced recently. He had a team member tell him that when she would speak up about how things were going. The supervisor and team leaders would not listen. They instead focused on what mistakes had been made to find more fault with her work performance or give advice as if they knew best just because of their position within the management structure.

He tried asking this person why it seemed like no one cared whether anything good happened at all. The answer: "They're never positive." When he pressed further by asking more questions. This situation shows that a relationship was never formed and when your only interaction is negative, people quit because that's what happened in this situation.

I have been on both sides of the equation, and negativity breeds turnover because I have misjudged people and have been misjudged. When no relationship is formed, then the gas tank is already empty.

CHAPTER SEVEN: THE IMPORTANCE OF BUILDING TRUST

Trust is another essential element of retaining employees. When employees trust their

Another important thing you can do to reduce turnover is to build trust with your employees. When people feel they can trust their boss, they are less likely to look for new opportunities elsewhere.

There are a few things you can do to build trust with your employees:

- Be honest with them. Don't try to hide things or mislead them.

- Be transparent in your decision-making. Let them know why you're making the decisions you're making.

- Follow through on your commitments.

Trust is another critical factor in employee retention. Employees who don't trust you are less likely to stay with the company.

There are a few things you can do to build trust with your employees:

- Be honest with them. Don't try to hide things from them or make promises you can't keep.

- Follow through on your commitments. If you say you're going to do something, do it.

- Be consistent in your words and actions. Employees need to know they can rely on you.

- Keep your confidences. Don't share information that should be kept private.

When we look at trust, Brad had a significantly lower turnover percentage than the average in transportation because he would not lie to his employees. In the transportation industry, you can lose trust quickly with employees if they don't trust you. Brad became an open book and would go the extra mile to sell drivers and other employees that if the employees worked with him, he would return the favor. This created a trusting relationship because too many lies to employees or left out the truth.

Michael hired two team members and told them from the start they would be working was seven days a week. Michael did not know how long it would last but he was honest with them. Both team members thanked him for being honest with them. These two team members worked very well and would report problems immediately to leadership before they became more significant problems. These two team members had great attendance and were hired directly to the company. This shows the importance of building trust and being upfront with people. We all know companies and people that lie to get people in, and shockingly, they have higher than average turnover.

Building trust with your employees is essential to reducing turnover. Be honest with them, follow through on your commitments, and

keep their confidence. When you build trust, you

create a foundation for a lasting relationship.

CHAPTER EIGHT: THE IMPORTANCE OF CREATING THE RIGHT ATMOSPHERE

The atmosphere at work can have a big impact on employee retention. If the environment is positive and supportive, employees are more likely to stay.

There are a few things you can do to create the right atmosphere:

- Encourage open communication. Create an environment where employees feel comfortable sharing their ideas and concerns.

- Promote collaboration. Encourage employees to work together to solve problems.

- Celebrate successes. Recognize and reward employees for a job well done.

- show empathy. Let your employees know you understand their challenges and are there to help them.

Creating the right atmosphere at work is essential to retaining employees. Employees are more likely to stay when the environment is positive and supportive.

Open communication is essential to creating the right atmosphere at work. Employees need to feel like they can share their ideas and concerns without fear of retribution. This can be done by encouraging open communication, promoting collaboration, and celebrating successes.

Encouraging open communication means creating an environment where employees feel comfortable sharing their ideas and concerns. This can be done by holding regular meetings where employees can share their thoughts, setting up an anonymous suggestion box, or Encouraging open communication is essential to creating the right workplace atmosphere. Employees need to feel like they can share their ideas and concerns without fear of retribution. This can be done by encouraging open communication is essential to creating the right atmosphere at work. Employees need to feel like they can share their ideas and concerns without fear of retribution. This can be done by encouraging open communication is essential to creating the right atmosphere at work. Employees need to feel like they can share their ideas and concerns without fear of retribution. This can be done by encouraging open communication is essential to creating the right atmosphere at work. Employees need to feel like they can share their ideas and concerns without fear of retribution. This can be done by

Promoting collaboration means encouraging employees to work together to solve problems. This can be done by holding team-building exercises; encouraging open communication is essential to creating the right workplace atmosphere. Employees need to feel like they can share their ideas and concerns without fear of retribution. This can be done by encouraging open communication is essential to creating the right atmosphere at work. Employees need to feel like they can share their ideas and concerns without fear of retribution. This can be done by encouraging open communication is essential to creating the right atmosphere at work. Employees need to feel like they can share their ideas and concerns without fear of retribution. This can be done by encouraging open communication is essential to creating the right atmosphere at work. Employees need to feel like they can share their ideas and concerns without fear of retribution. This can be done by celebrating successes means recognizing and rewarding employees for a job well done. This can be done by giving employees verbal praise, sending thank-you notes, or giving employees a raise or bonus.

Show empathy by letting your employees know you understand their challenges and are there to help them. This can be done by listening to their concerns, offering support, and providing resources.

Creating the right atmosphere at work is essential to retaining employees. Employees are more likely to stay when the environment is positive and supportive. These tips will help you create the right atmosphere and improve employee retention.

When we look at the right atmosphere, Brad has been in good and bad environments. When you look at the principles he has talked about, it is easy to see how those would lead to a good or bad environment. If you want to create a good environment at work, then you should focus on the following: open communication, promoting collaboration, celebrating successes, and showing empathy. Let's take a closer look at each of these principles.

Open communication is key to creating the right atmosphere. Employees need to feel like they can share their ideas and concerns without fear of retribution. This can be done by holding regular meetings where employees can share their thoughts, setting up an anonymous suggestion box, or encouraging open communication is essential to creating the right workplace atmosphere. Employees need to feel like they can share their ideas and concerns without fear of retribution. This can be done by encouraging open communication is essential to creating the right atmosphere at work. Employees need to feel like they can share their ideas and concerns without fear of retribution. This can be done by encouraging open communication is essential to creating the right atmosphere at work. Employees need to feel like they can share their ideas and concerns without fear of retribution. This can be done by encouraging open communication is essential to creating the right atmosphere at work. Employees need to feel like they can share their ideas and concerns without fear of retribution. This can be done by

Promoting collaboration is another way to create the right atmosphere. This means encouraging employees to work together to solve problems. This can be done by holding team-building exercises; encouraging open communication is essential to creating the right workplace atmosphere. Employees need to feel like they can share their ideas and concerns without fear of retribution. This can be done by encouraging open communication is essential to creating the right atmosphere at work. Employees need to feel like they can share their ideas and concerns without fear of retribution. This can be done by encouraging open communication is essential to creating the right atmosphere at work. Employees need to feel like they can share their ideas and concerns without fear of retribution.

When we look at these concepts, it points at communication, collaboration, celebrating successes, and showing empathy.

Brad has seen many projects and teams fail due to a lack of effective communication. When communication is not clear, then, things fail.

These are the most critical parts of retention are communication and empathy. If you cannot put yourself in another's shoes and understand that their house is burning, and they need to leave, then you have sold yourself on failure as a human being. He has seen collaboration go too far and end up with too many meaningless meetings, so make sure what you have to say is really important to a project, not just your ego. Celebrating successes is something he has watched because when you accomplish something significant, a celebration helps morale. On the other side, an email with 100 replies to a birthday is just flat out too much.

Michael has watched companies that would not train their employees. Reports came back from team members saying they had been shown maybe once or twice, then placed on the job and left to figure things out themselves with no supervision whatsoever by management--and this is after just two days! The trainer never showed up again as promised until six months later when he suddenly appeared out of nowhere one day without any warning whatsoever-which shocked several people who were still there working patiently through all sorts of problems because nobody else seemed caring enough anymore...

So this organization did nothing to create a positive environment and did way more to create a negative one

In conclusion, any organization must utilize selling techniques to improve employee engagement and retention. By creating an open and collaborative atmosphere, you can encourage employees to stay with your company for the long term. You can show employees that you are invested in their success by showing you care. And by practicing empathy and communication.

CHAPTER NINE: THE IMPORTANCE OF MOVING AWAY FROM AUTHORITARIAN LEADERSHIP

Employees are less likely to stay with a company if they feel like an authoritarian leader controls them. This type of leadership creates a feeling of insecurity and mistrust.

There are a few things you can do to move away from authoritarian leadership:

- Encourage employee input. Ask for their ideas and opinions on decisions.

- Give employees autonomy. Allow them to make decisions and take actions without your approval.

- Delegate authority. Empower employees to make decisions in their areas of responsibility.

- Support employees. Let them know you are there to help them succeed.

Leadership styles have changed throughout the years as organizations have become more complex. The traditional, top-down leadership style is no longer effective in today's environment. Authoritarian leaders are not as successful in retaining employees because they create a feeling of insecurity and mistrust.

Encouraging employee input is one way to move away from an authoritarian leadership style. Asking for their ideas and opinions on decisions shows that you value their input. Giving employees autonomy is another way to empower them to make decisions and take action without your approval. This allows them to feel like they are part of the decision-making process.

Delegating authority is another way to support employees and let them know you are there to help them succeed.

Organizations that move away from an authoritarian leadership style are more successful in retaining employees. You can create a more positive work environment by empowering employees to make decisions and supporting their success.

This chapter should not even be necessary because authoritarian leadership only breeds negativity. You are not selling anyone with an authoritarian leadership style, and data shows this approach is ineffective in today's world, so this should be an easy fix.

Managers think they are weak because they are not being assertive and showing their authority, this is a personal issue. These managers and not leaders are a dying breed unless you are in the military or playing organized sports. Brad has watched so many authoritarian leaders fail over time, and the worst part is they blame others and never look inward at their failures.

Michael knew one supervisor that would ask for employees' feedback and ideas. This whole department progressed; team members were happy and said they felt part of a team, and it was good to know that the supervisor valued their ideas. The same supervisor had failed multiple times previously because he was an authoritarian manager and did not become a leader until he abandoned the authoritarian style.

The importance of moving away from an authoritarian leadership style cannot be understated. This type of leadership creates a feeling of insecurity and mistrust among employees. To retain employees, it is important to encourage employee input, give them autonomy, delegate authority, and support them. These practices will create a more positive work environment and lead to more tremendous success in retaining employees.

Learn to sell your employees on the mission, and they will respond accordingly.

CHAPTER TEN: THE IMPORTANCE OF IMPROVING LISTENING SKILLS

Listening is an essential skill for all leaders. If you want to keep your employees, you must listen to them.

There are a few things you can do to improve your listening skills:

- Give employees your full attention. Don't try to multitask when they are talking to you.

- Listen for understanding. Ask questions to make sure you understand what they are saying.

- Listen for feelings. Pay attention to the emotions behind the words.

- Respect employees' opinions. Don't dismiss their ideas out of hand.

Listening is a critical skill for leaders. If you want to retain your employees, it is important to listen to them. Employees want to feel like their voices are heard and that their opinions matter.

When you are talking to an employee, give them your full attention. Don't try to multitask. This sends the message that you are not really interested in what they have to say. Listen for understanding and ask questions if you need clarification. It is also important to listen for feelings. Pay attention to the emotions behind the words. This will help you understand how the employee is feeling.

Respect employees' opinions and don't dismiss their ideas out of hand. Showing that you value their input will go a long way toward engendering loyalty and commitment.

If you want to keep your employees, it is essential to listen to them. By showing that you value their input, you can create a more positive work environment and improve retention.

Michael and I have spoken with many managers over the last year who they didn't listen to anyone. They call to speak with us and then do not listen to anything, so their minds are already made up. They are sold because they will not listen and understand they have two ears and one mouth for a reason.

When it comes to employee retention, one of the most important things a leader can do is to improve their listening skills. Listening is a key part of building trust and relationships with employees, and it shows that you value their input.

There are a few things you can do to improve your listening skills:

- Give employees your full attention. Don't try to multitask when they are talking to you.

- Listen for understanding. Ask questions to make sure you understand what they are saying.

- Listen for feelings. Pay attention to the emotions behind the words.

- Respect employees' opinions. Don't dismiss their ideas out of hand.

By showing employees that you respect their opinions and listening to what they have to say, you can create a more positive work environment and improve retention.

CHAPTER ELEVEN: THE IMPORTANCE OF LEARNING SELLING TECHNIQUES

Selling techniques can be used to improve employee retention. By using these techniques, you can keep your employees engaged and motivated.

In any business, employee retention is vital to success. A high turnover rate can be costly and disruptive, so it's important to do what you can to keep your employees happy and engaged. One way to do this is by providing training in selling techniques. By teaching your employees how to sell effectively, you'll not only help them be more successful in their roles, but you'll also give them the skills they need to succeed in other aspects of their lives. In addition, studies have shown that employees who feel like they have the opportunity to grow and develop are more likely to stick around. So, if you're looking for ways to improve employee retention, learning selling techniques is a great place to start.

In today's competitive job market, retaining good employees is essential to the success of any business. One way to help ensure that your employees stay with your company is to provide them with the skills they need to be successful in their roles. This includes teaching them how to sell effectively.

While some people are natural salespeople, others may need some help honing their skills.

Fortunately, there are a number of resources available to help employees learn how to sell more effectively. By taking advantage of these resources, you can give your employees the tools they need to succeed in their roles and keep them from leaving your company for greener pastures.

There are a few things you can do to learn selling techniques:

- Read books on selling. There are many great resources available.

- Take a course on selling. This will allow you to practice the techniques.

- Attend a seminar on selling. Seminars are a great way to learn from experts in the field.

- Hire a coach. A coach can help you learn and implement selling techniques.

Top selling skills that you should improve on for employee retention are:

1. Confidence - maintaining a positive attitude about your organization and what you have to offer an employee.

When it comes to employee retention, one of the most important things a leader can do is to be confident. Showing confidence in your organization and what it has to offer will go a long way toward keeping employees engaged and motivated.

There are a few things you can do to show confidence:

- Believe in your products or services. If you don't believe in them, why should your employees?

- Be positive. Talk about the good things happening in your company.

- Be optimistic. Things may not always go perfectly, but employees will be more likely to stick around if they think you believe things will improve.

By being confident and showing faith in your company, you can improve employee retention.

2. Resilience - communicating with conviction

Convincing your employees of the importance of their work and how it fits into the company's goals can go a long way toward improving retention. When employees feel like they are part of something larger, they are more likely to stick around.

There are a few things you can do to communicate with conviction:

- Be clear about the company's goals. Employees need to know where the company is headed and how their work fits into that picture.

- Be passionate about your work. If you're not excited about what you're doing, employees will pick up on that.

- Be honest. Don't try to sell your employees on something that isn't true.

Communicating with conviction will help you improve employee retention.

Enthusiasm is contagious. When you're excited about what you're doing, employees will pick up on that and be more likely to get excited themselves.

There are a few things you can do to show enthusiasm:

> - Be positive. Talk about the good things happening in your company.

- Be passionate about your work. If you're

not excited about what you're doing,

employees will pick up on that.

- Be encouraging. Let your employees

know that you believe in them and their

ability to succeed.

Showing enthusiasm will help you improve

employee retention.

3. Active listening - understanding the employee's needs

Active listening is a crucial skill for anyone

in a leadership position. When you can really

listen to what your employees are saying, it shows

that you care about them and their needs. This can

go a long way toward improving employee retention.

There are a few things you can do to improve your active listening skills:

- Pay attention. When someone is speaking, make sure you're giving them your full attention.

- Listen with your body. Nod your head or make other affirmative gestures to let the person know you're following along.

- Repeat back what you've heard. This will help ensure that you've understood what the person is saying.

By improving your active listening skills, you can improve employee retention.

4. Rapport building - selling your personality

Building rapport with your employees is important for several reasons. First, it helps you get to know them on a personal level. This can make them more likely to trust and respect you. Second, it gives you an opportunity to sell them on your personality. If they like you as a person, they're more likely to want to work with you.

There are a few things you can do to build rapport with your employees:

- Get to know them on a personal level. Ask about their families, their hobbies, and anything else that's important to them.

- Be genuine. Don't try to be someone you're not. Employees will see through that and it will damage your rapport.

- Show interest in what they're saying. This will help them feel valued and appreciated. Building rapport with your employees can improve employee retention.

5. Continual Self-Improvement

Continual self-improvement is important for anyone in a leadership position. When you're constantly working to improve your skills, employees will take notice. They'll see that you're dedicated to being the best leader you can be and that you're willing to invest in yourself. This can go a long way toward improving employee retention.

There are a few things you can do to improve your skills:

- Read books on leadership. This will help you learn new techniques and strategies.

- Attend workshops and seminars. These can provide you with an opportunity to network with other leaders and learn from their experiences.

- Hire a coach. A coach can help you identify areas where you need improvement and give you specific advice on how to improve.

By continually improving your skills, you can improve employee retention. In conclusion, there are many selling techniques that can be used to improve employee retention. By showing

enthusiasm, practicing active listening, building

rapport, and continually improving your skills, you

can create a positive working environment that

employees will want to be a part of.

CHAPTER TWELVE: THE IMPORTANCE OF PROVIDING VALUE TO EMPLOYEES

Employees need to feel like they are getting value from their job. They will be less likely to stay with the company if they don't.

There are a few things you can do to provide value to employees:

- Pay them a competitive salary. Employees need to feel like they are being compensated fairly.

- Offer benefits and perks. These can help attract and retain employees.

- Give them growth opportunities. Employees need to feel like they are progressing in their careers.

- Invest in their development. Provide training and development opportunities so they can improve their skills.

Employees need to feel like they are getting value from their job. If they don't, they will be less likely to stay with the company. There are a few things you can do to provide value to employees:

-Pay them a competitive salary. Employees need to feel like they are being compensated fairly.

-Offer benefits and perks. These can help attract and retain employees.

-Give them growth opportunities. Employees need to feel like they are progressing in their careers.

-Invest in their development. Provide training and development opportunities so they can improve their skills.

By providing value to employees, you can create a more positive work environment and improve retention. When employees feel valued, they are more likely to be engaged and motivated. This leads to a decrease in turnover and an increase in productivity.

It is important to invest in your employees. By doing so, you are showing that you value their skills and experience. This will help them feel appreciated and will make them more likely to stay with the company. Training and development opportunities are also significant. They allow employees to learn new skills and improve their existing ones. This helps them feel like they are growing in their career, which is a major factor in employee engagement and retention.

Providing value to employees is an essential part of retaining them. By paying them a competitive salary, offering benefits and perks, and investing in their development, you can create a positive work environment and decrease turnover.

As any manager knows, happy employees are productive employees. When workers feel valued and appreciated, they are more likely to be engaged with their work and committed to their company. This leads to a decrease in turnover and an increase in productivity. There are a number of ways to show employees that they are valued. Providing training and development opportunities shows that you are invest in their growth and development. Offering competitive salaries and benefits demonstrates that you are committed to attracting and retaining the best talent. And making time for regular one-on-one check-ins sends the message that you care about their well-being. By taking steps to create a positive work environment, you can improve retention and increase productivity.

Employee retention is essential to the success of the company. Not only does it reduce the costs associated with recruiting and training new employees, but it also helps to foster a positive work environment. One way to improve employee retention is to provide value to employees. This can be in the form of monetary compensation, but it can also take the form of non-monetary perks, such as flexible hours or paid time off. When employees feel valued, they are more likely to be engaged and motivated. This leads to a decrease in turnover and an increase in productivity. In today's competitive job market, providing value to employees is more critical than ever. By taking steps to improve employee retention, businesses can create a more positive work environment and position themselves for long-term success.

CHAPTER THIRTEEN: THE IMPORTANCE OF ADDING SELF-DEVELOPMENT OPPORTUNITIES

Self-development opportunities can help improve employee retention. These opportunities allow employees to grow and develop, making them more likely to stay with the company.

There are a few things you can do to add self-development opportunities:

- Offer mentoring programs. These programs pair employees with more experienced employees who can help them develop their skills.

- Provide training and development opportunities. This can include online courses, seminars, and workshops.

- Encourage employees to pursue their goals. Support employees as they strive to reach their goals.

- Invest in their future. Help employees plan for their future by providing financial planning assistance.

Self-development opportunities can help improve employee retention. These opportunities give employees the chance to grow and develop, which makes them more likely to stay with the company.

Mentoring programs are a great way to provide self-development opportunities. These programs pair employees with more experienced employees who can help them develop their skills.

This is a beneficial opportunity for both parties; the mentee gets guidance and support, while the mentor gets the satisfaction of helping someone grow.

Training and development opportunities are another way to add self-development opportunities. This can include online courses, seminars, and workshops. These opportunities allow employees to learn new skills and improve their existing ones. They also give employees the chance to network with other professionals.

Encouraging employees to pursue their goals is another way to add self-development opportunities. Support employees as they strive to reach their goals. This helps them feel motivated and supported, which makes them more likely to stay with the company.

Investing in their future is the last way to add self-development opportunities. Help employees plan for their future by providing financial planning assistance. This will help them feel secure in their future, which will make them more likely to stay with the company.

Self-development opportunities are a great way to improve employee retention. By offering mentoring programs, training and development opportunities, and investing in their future, you can show employees that you value their growth and development. This will make them more likely to stay with the company and not leave you for the competition.

By utilizing these selling techniques, you can improve employee engagement and retention. Creating the right atmosphere, moving away from authoritarian leadership, improving listening skills, learning selling techniques, providing value to employees, and adding self-development opportunities.

A successful business is built on a foundation of strong employees. To attract and retain top talent, it is essential to provide opportunities for professional development. Employees who feel that their skills are being utilized and given opportunities to grow are more likely to be engaged in their work and less likely to look for new opportunities elsewhere.

Additionally, businesses that invest in their employees' development are more likely to foster a culture of innovation and creativity. When employees feel empowered to develop new skills and improve upon their existing ones, they are more likely to come up with creative solutions to challenges and contribute to the overall success of the organization. Therefore, adding self-development opportunities to your employee benefits package is an investment that will pay off in both the short and long term.

Most managers know that happy employees are key to a successful business. Not only are they more productive, but they're also more likely to stick around. That's why it's so important to offer self-development opportunities to your team. When employees feel like they're learning and growing, they're more satisfied with their job - and less likely to look for new opportunities elsewhere.

There are a number of ways to provide self-development opportunities for your team. You can offer classes or workshops, sponsor educational events, or create internal mentorship programs. You can also simply encourage employees to take advantage of resources like online courses or industry-specific books and articles. No matter how you do it, making self-development a priority will pay off in increased employee satisfaction -

and retention.

CONCLUSION

The bottom line is that selling techniques can be extremely useful for businesses who are looking to improve employee engagement and retention. By focusing on key selling points, such as relationship building, trust, communication, and providing value to employees, organizations can create a more positive and productive work environment. In turn, this will lead to higher levels of employee engagement and retention, which will save the organization money and increase productivity.

For any business, employee engagement and retention are key. After all, happy employees mean satisfied customers, which leads to increased profits. There are a number of selling techniques that can be used to improve employee engagement and retention. For example, relationship building is key. Employees who feel like they have a good relationship with their boss are more likely to be engaged and committed to their job. Trust is also important. Employees who feel like they can trust their boss are more likely to be engaged and productive. Communication is another key selling point. Bosses who take the time to communicate with their employees are more likely to build trust and foster a positive relationship. Finally, providing value to employees is essential. Employees who feel like they are valued by their company are more likely to be engaged and productive. By focusing on these key selling points, businesses can create a more positive and productive work environment, leading to higher levels of employee engagement and retention.

The bottom line is that selling techniques can be beneficial for businesses that are looking to improve employee engagement and retention. By focusing on key selling points, such as relationship building, trust, communication, and providing value to employees, organizations can create a more positive and productive work environment. This will lead to higher levels of employee engagement and retention, saving the organization money and increasing productivity. Therefore, it is important for businesses to consider using selling techniques to improve employee engagement and retention. When done correctly, selling techniques can have a positive impact on the organization.

Below are the selling techniques for employee retention. Please contact us for onsite training to establish a program for your organization.

Selling Techniques for Retention

1. Relationship Building- To keep your employees, you have to build a good rapport and relationship with them. This can be done by regularly communicating with them, being transparent, and create a positive work environment.

2. Build Trust with Employees- It is essential that your employees trust you for them to stay with the company. You can build trust by being honest, keeping promises, and following through on commitments.

3. Create the Right Atmosphere- The workplace's atmosphere can either make or break employee morale. Make sure to create a positive work environment conducive to productivity and creativity.

4. Back Away from Authoritarian Leadership- A top-down leadership style can often lead to employee disengagement. Instead, adopt a more collaborative leadership style that allows employees to have a say in decision-making.

5. Improve Listening Skills- One of the most critical selling techniques is learning how to listen to your employees. This will help you understand their needs and concerns and address them accordingly.

6. Learn Selling Techniques- To improve employee retention, it is important to learn effective selling techniques. This includes understanding the customer's needs, building rapport, and closing the sale.

7. Provide Value to Employees- Another way to keep your employees is by providing them value. This can be in the form of competitive salaries, benefits, and development opportunities.

8. Add Self-Development Opportunities-
Employees are often more engaged when they feel
like they are constantly learning and growing.
Offer self-development opportunities such as
training, mentorship, and educational resources.

The bottom line is that selling techniques
can be beneficial for businesses that are looking to
improve employee engagement and retention. By
focusing on key selling points, such as relationship
building, trust, communication, and providing
value to employees, organizations can create a
more positive and productive work environment.
In turn, this will lead to higher levels of employee
engagement and retention, which will save the
organization money and increase productivity.

If you are interested in learning more about how to utilize selling techniques to improve employee engagement and retention, check out our book. This book will provide you with all the information you need to start implementing these techniques in your organization. With our help, you can make employee engagement and retention a top priority in your company. Contact us today to learn more and being implementing the concepts of the book into your organization.

Thanks, from Brad and Michael, AKA: The Self Development Factory.

brad@selfdevelopmentfactory.com

michael@selfdevelopmentfactory.com

www.selfdevelopmentfactory.com